What's Going to Happen?

Making Your Hypothesis

Paul Challen

Science educational consultant: Suzy Gazlay

Crabtree Publishing Company

www.crabtreebooks.com

Crabtree Publishing Company

www.crabtreebooks.com

Author: Paul Challen
Series editor: Vashti Gwynn
Editorial director: Paul Humphrey
Editor: Adrianna Morganelli
Proofreader: Reagan Miller
Production coordinator: Katherine Berti
Prepress technician: Katherine Berti
Project manager: Kathy Middleton
Illustration: Stefan Chabluk and Stuart Harrison
Photography: Chris Fairclough
Cover design: Katherine Berti
Design: sprout.uk.com
Photo research: Vashti Gwynn

Produced for Crabtree Publishing Company by Discovery Books.

Thanks to models Ottilie and Sorcha Austin-Baker, Dan Brice-Bateman, Matthew Morris, and Amrit and Tara Shoker.

Photographs and Illustrations:
Barbara Bedell: p. 25 (right)
Corbis: Bettmann: p. 25 (left)
Getty Images: Robert Harding: p. 4 (bottom left); SSPL: p. 6 (left); National Geographic/David Doubilet: p. 8 (center); Richard Lewisohn: p. 10; Spencer Platt: p. 11;
Image Source: p. 20 (bottom); Hulton Archive: p. 21 (left); Peter Dazeley: p. 26
Istockphoto: Nikitje: p. 7 (center); Hulton Archive: p. 13 (bottom right); Diloute: p. 28
NASA: p. 14 (left)
Samara Parent: back cover, p. 1 (top)
Science Photo Library: p. 16
Shutterstock: cover, p. 1 (center left and center right), 3 (center), 7 (top left), 8 (center left), 12 (left), 13 (bottom left), 16 (center right), 20 (center left), 21 (top right), 29 (bottom); HD Connelly: p. 12 (right); Ali Ender Birer: p. 15 (top); Liv Friis-Larsen: p. 24; Yarchyk: p. 27 (top)

Library and Archives Canada Cataloguing in Publication

Challen, Paul, 1967-
What's going to happen? Making your hypothesis / Paul Challen.

(Step into science)
Includes index.
ISBN 978-0-7787-5157-1 (bound).--ISBN 978-0-7787-5172-4 (pbk.)

1. Science--Methodology--Juvenile literature. 2. Science--Experiments--Juvenile literature. 3. Hypothesis--Juvenile literature. I. Title. II. Series: Step into science (St. Catharines, Ont.)

Q175.2.C44 2010   j507.8   C2009-906462-6

Library of Congress Cataloging-in-Publication Data

Challen, Paul C. (Paul Clarence), 1967-
What's going to happen? Making your hypothesis / Paul Challen.
p. cm. -- (Step into science)
Includes index.
ISBN 978-0-7787-5157-1 (reinforced lib. bdg. : alk. paper)
-- ISBN 978-0-7787-5172-4 (pbk. : alk. paper)
1. Science--Methodology--Juvenile literature. 2. Hypothesis--Juvenile literature. I. Title. II. Series.

Q175.2.C4274 2010
507.8--dc22
2009044174

Crabtree Publishing Company

www.crabtreebooks.com   1-800-387-7650

Printed in Canada/042011/KR20110304

Published in Canada
Crabtree Publishing
616 Welland Ave.
St. Catharines, Ontario
L2M 5V6

Published in the United States
Crabtree Publishing
PMB 59051
350 Fifth Avenue, 59th Floor
New York, New York 10118

Published in the United Kingdom
Crabtree Publishing
Maritime House
Basin Road North, Hove
BN41 1WR

Published in Australia
Crabtree Publishing
386 Mt. Alexander Rd.
Ascot Vale (Melbourne)
VIC 3032

CONTENTS

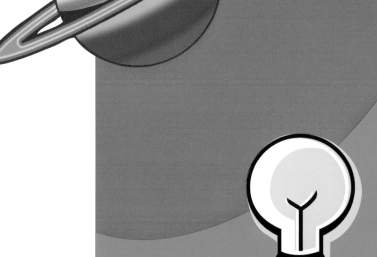

THE SCIENTIFIC METHOD

Have you ever been in an elevator? The **scientific method** is like an elevator—you enter at the first floor and take the elevator up. The elevator passes one floor at a time, and you get closer and closer to your final stop. Sometimes, however, the journey takes you back down before you continue on to reach your destination.

In the same way, following each step in the scientific method is important for making scientific discoveries. Sometimes, though, scientists have to stop, go back, and think again before they continue.

In this book, we will look at step two of the scientific method. When scientists ask themselves "what's going to happen?" they are not just guessing. Instead, they make what is called a hypothesis. A hypothesis is a **prediction** about what an experiment will prove. The important thing about a hypothesis is that it is based on facts. know about their subject to make their hypothesis.

◄ This scientist is studying volcanoes. His data will show whether his hypothesis is correct or not.

Beginning Your Scientific Investigation

Be curious! Questions can come from anywhere, anytime. Questions help scientists make **observations** and do **research**. Science is all about problem-solving!

Making Your Hypothesis

So, what is next? You have a question, and you have done some research. You think you know what will happen when you perform your experiment. The term *hypothesis* means educated guess. So, make a guess and get started!

Designing Your Experiment

How are you going to test your hypothesis? Designing a safe, accurate experiment will give **results** that answer your question.

Collecting and Recording Your Data

During an experiment, scientists make careful observations and record exactly what happens.

Displaying and Understanding Results

Now your **data** can be organized into **graphs**, **charts**, and diagrams. These help you read the information, think about it, and figure out what it means.

Making Conclusions and Answering the Question

So, what did you learn during your experiment? Did your data prove your hypothesis? Scientists share their results so other scientists can try out the experiment, or use the results to try another experiment.

WHY MAKE A HYPOTHESIS?

Why is one of the first steps in the scientific method to make a hypothesis? A hypothesis helps scientists to focus their experiments. It helps them to choose the particular things they would like to test.

A hypothesis also helps scientists think about the kinds of experiments they will do to investigate their questions. It tells them exactly what they need their experiments to prove or disprove.

Don't lose focus! Create a hypothesis!

What am I?
People have studied how the world works for thousands of years. For a long time, these people were called natural **philosophers**, or men of science. It wasn't until 1833 that the word "scientist" was used. It was created by a man named William Whewell (left). Whewell studied many different kinds of science, including **physics**, **astronomy**, and **geology**.

There are many different experiments you could do with plants. The experiments would show you slightly different things. That's why it's important to make a focused hypothesis.

For instance, you might have been thinking about plants and sunlight, but you can't create an experiment out of that! First you would have to focus your hypothesis.

For example, you might say, "I think that plants grow faster with more sunlight." Now that's a hypothesis you can plan an experiment around!

WHAT DO YOU KNOW?

The important thing to remember about making a hypothesis is that it really is a guess based on knowledge. To make this kind of guess, scientists use everything they know about their question.

The Shark Lady

Dr. Eugenie Clark is a scientist who studies poisonous fish and sharks. She discovered that a fish called the Moses Sole made a white liquid inside its body. The fish releases the liquid when threatened. Clark discovered that the liquid made her fingers tingle when she touched it. Based on her observation, she made a hypothesis that the liquid might work as a shark repellent—and it did!

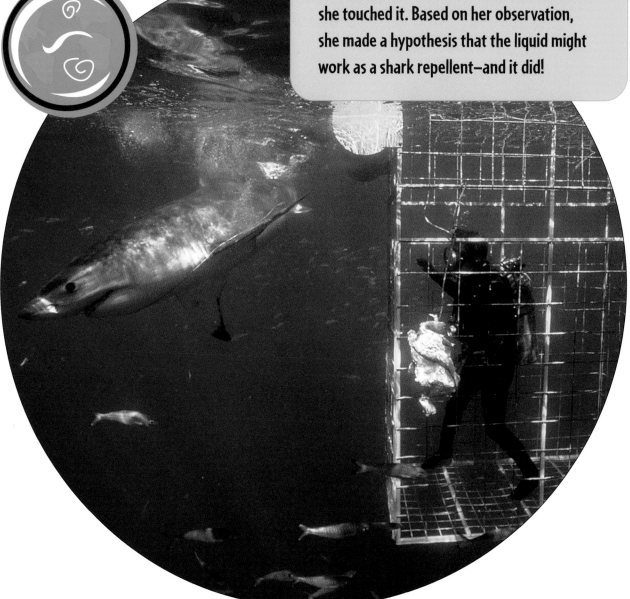

► Saying that a ball will fall if you drop it might seem obvious. It's still a real hypothesis though. This girl has just proved it right!

They can think about other experiments they've done or heard about. They can think about things they've learned from books, the Internet, or other scientists. They can also think about observations they've made about the world.

Imagine if you held a ball up in the air and let go. It's probably easy for you to make a hypothesis about what would happen! You have seen a ball fall to the ground before. This means your hypothesis would be "the ball will fall to the ground." You just made an educated guess!

FINDING INFORMATION

How do scientists get information to help them make a hypothesis?

Most scientists look in books, do research on the Internet, or talk to other people about their question. Also, scientists know how to break down the different parts of an experiment. This can help them make a hypothesis.

▼ This young scientist is finding out about science in his school library. His knowledge will help him make good hypotheses in the future.

▲ What will happen when this soccer player kicks the ball and it hits the wall? You can think about the two different parts of this question. This will help you make a hypothesis.

For example, suppose you did not know what would happen if you kicked a soccer ball against a wall. You could break the question down into two parts. First, you could do some research on what happens to a ball when it is kicked. Second, you could investigate what happens when a ball hits a wall. Now you know about both steps of the problem.

You are ready to make a hypothesis about what would happen if you kicked the ball *and* it hit a wall.

MAKING A HYPOTHESIS

Once you have pulled together all the information you can about the parts of your experiment, it is time to make your hypothesis. How do you do that?

Imagine you're going to find out what happens when you put a sugar cube in hot water. You might never have done this before. But maybe you've seen your parents put sugar in their coffee. You could think about what happens to the sugar in the coffee. Then you could imagine what might happen to sugar in hot water.

> ▶ Imagine what would happen to these sugar cubes if they were put in the hot coffee. Does it help you make a hypothesis?

Can you rise to a challenge like Archimedes?

Archimedes

Archimedes (below) was a Greek scientist who lived thousands of years ago. He wanted to find a way to measure the **volume** of an object. Volume is how much space an object takes up. It can be hard to measure if the object is an odd shape. One day he noticed that when he got into the bath, the water level rose a bit. This was because he was taking up space where the water had been. Using his imagination, he realized that the same thing would happen if he put any other object into water. If he did this, he could measure how much the water level went up. From that, he could calculate the volume of the object he'd put in!

Your hypothesis needs to be a **statement**. A statement is when you say that something is definitely going to happen, or do something, or be a certain way. In this case you would say, "I hypothesize that hot water makes sugar **dissolve**." Make sure your hypothesis is a statement you will be able to prove or disprove.

GUESS AGAIN!

Now you might be wondering what happens if your experiment proves your hypothesis is wrong.

In fact, it does not matter if your hypothesis is incorrect. Remember that making a hypothesis is just a way to get the experiment started. It gets you thinking about how the experiment *might* turn out.

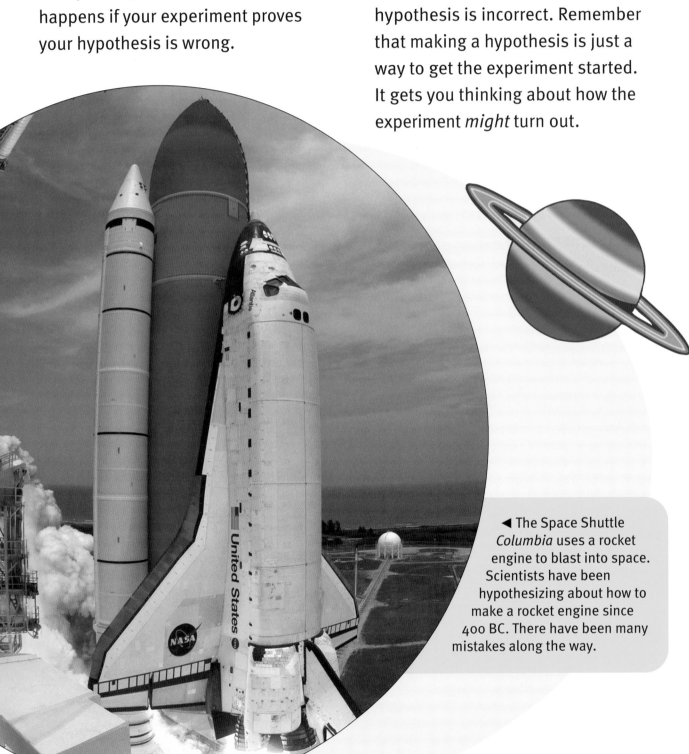

◀ The Space Shuttle *Columbia* uses a rocket engine to blast into space. Scientists have been hypothesizing about how to make a rocket engine since 400 BC. There have been many mistakes along the way.

▲ This photo was taken from space. You can clearly see that Earth is curved. But before we could take photos like these, scientists found it difficult to figure out what shape Earth might be.

Aristotle deserves a "round" of applause for proving his hypothesis that Earth is shaped like a sphere.

Aristotle

For a long time, there were different hypotheses about the shape of Earth. Some scientists thought it was a flat **disk**. Some thought it was a flat square. Some even thought it was a cylinder! Then in 330 BC, the Greek thinker Aristotle made an important observation. He traveled south to places like Cyprus and Egypt. He realized he could see different stars in these countries from the stars he could see from back home. Based on this observation, he made a hypothesis that Earth was curved.

SLOW SCIENCE

It's important to make a hypothesis that can be tested in an experiment. A hypothesis cannot become a fact until it is proved.

Sometimes, though, a scientist may think something works a certain way but he or she can't test it. This might be because he or she doesn't have the technology to do the experiment. It might be because the experiment would be too difficult or dangerous. It could also be because he or she can't get enough data to prove the hypothesis.

Poor Wegener! It seems no one got his "drift."

Jigsaw Earth

Alfred Wegener (below right) was a German scientist. He noticed that Earth's **continents** all looked like they could fit together. In 1915, he hypothesized that millions of years ago they had started off as one big piece of land. He thought that they had begun to drift apart long before humans were around. But Wegener was unable to show proof of his hypothesis, and other scientists argued against it very strongly. They could not see how it could happen. Wegener died in 1930, but it wasn't until the 1960s that other scientists started to think he was right. His hypothesis is now a **theory** called continental drift.

This means that some hypotheses can take a long time to prove. Some might never be proved at all! In the meantime, other people may not believe the scientist's hypothesis.

Sometimes, there is lots of evidence to support a hypothesis, but no proof. In this case, the hypothesis becomes a theory. This means that scientists believe it is true, even though it hasn't been proved.

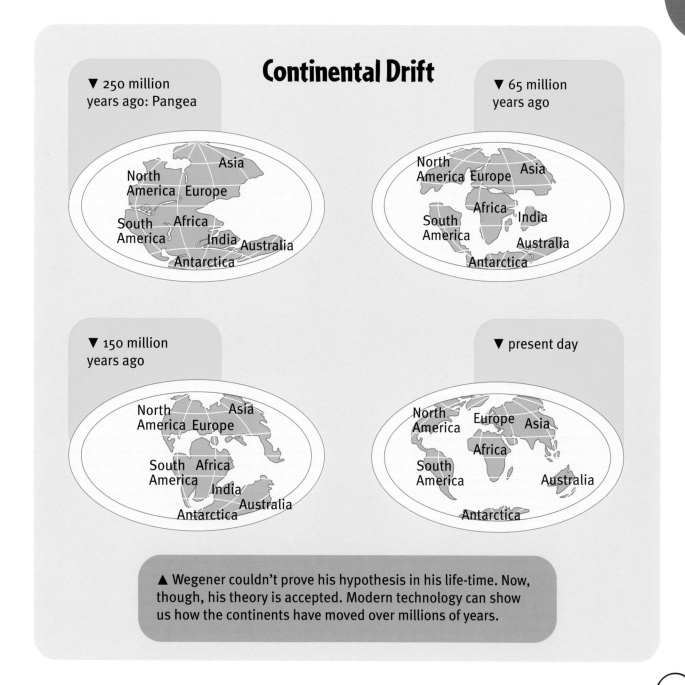

Continental Drift

▼ 250 million years ago: Pangea

▼ 65 million years ago

▼ 150 million years ago

▼ present day

▲ Wegener couldn't prove his hypothesis in his life-time. Now, though, his theory is accepted. Modern technology can show us how the continents have moved over millions of years.

LET'S EXPERIMENT!

Water Works

Problem

You've probably seen puddles dry up when the sun comes out. Why does this happen? Make a hypothesis first, then try this experiment.

Materials:

- ☑ three plastic cups that are the same size
- ☑ permanent marker
- ☑ water
- ☑ pen
- ☑ paper or journal

1 Fill your cups one-fourth of the way with water. On the inside of each cup, mark where the water level comes to with your marker.

2 Put one of your cups in the refrigerator.

3 Put one of your cups somewhere indoors. Choose somewhere not too hot, and not too cold.

4 Put the third cup somewhere warm, like near a radiator or heat vent. Make sure it's not really hot, or your cup will melt.

5 Check your cups in the morning and at night. Each time, make a mark where the water level comes to. Write down the date and time you make each mark on a piece of paper or in your **journal** (see pages 28-29).

6 Leave your cups for two or three days. Continue checking the cups twice a day. After this time, you can compare the measurements of each cup. Which cup has the least amount of water? Which cup has the most? What did you find out? Was your hypothesis correct?

I Hypothesize...

Do you have a clothes-dryer at home? If you do, you might have noticed that it doesn't use light to dry clothes. It uses heat. This is the kind of observation that might help you make a hypothesis about this experiment.

THE SHOCKING TRUTH!

The American scientist Benjamin Franklin did a famous experiment in 1752. This experiment is a great example of how a hypothesis helps shape an experiment.

People had known for a long time that electricity could move from one place to another. They weren't sure exactly how this happened.

Benjamin Franklin

Benjamin Franklin was born in Boston, Massachusetts in 1706. He loved to read as a young boy, and that helped him become one of the most important scientists of his day. Franklin was also a writer, **printer,** and one of the people that helped write the early laws of the United States.

▼ Benjamin Franklin found a dangerous way to test his hypothesis. It did prove him right, though!

Lightning Strike

Not everyone who has attempted to do Franklin's lightning experiment has been as lucky as Ben. In 1753, just a year after Franklin, a German scientist named Georg Wilhelm Richmann was killed when he tried to repeat the experiment.

Franklin had done some experiments with **static electricity**. Static electricity is what makes your hair stand up when you rub a balloon against it. Franklin hypothesized that lightning was a kind of static electricity. He thought that lightning might move from one object to another. To find out he tied an iron key to the end of a kite string and flew the kite during a storm. Lightning hit the kite and when Franklin put his hand near the key, an electric spark jumped from the key and gave him a shock! This showed that electricity had traveled from the kite, down the string, and into the key.

▲ Have you ever rubbed a balloon on your head and made all your hair stand up? If you have, it means you have already made some observations about static electricity!

LET'S EXPERIMENT!

Smooth Science

Problem

Some scientists design and build machines. Sometimes, they need parts of the machine to be extra rough or extra smooth. Smooth things move against other things more easily than rough things. Which of these—a shiny book, a pillowcase, and sandpaper—is smoothest? Remember to make a hypothesis.

Materials:

- ☑ a coin
- ☑ several thick books
- ☑ a shiny, hard-cover book
- ☑ a pillowcase
- ☑ a sheet of sandpaper
- ☑ tape
- ☑ a ruler
- ☑ a pencil
- ☑ a paper or journal

1 Make a pile with your thick books on a table. Lean the hard-cover book against the pile so it makes a ramp. The high end of the ramp should be about eight inches (20 cm) from the tabletop.

2 Place your coin at the top of the ramp, lying on its flat side. Now let go. Does the coin slide? Use your ruler to measure how far the coin travels. Record the measurement on your paper or in your journal.

3 Now put your hard-cover book into the pillowcase. Pull the pillowcase tightly underneath the book, so that it is smooth on top. Lean the book against the pile to create the ramp again. Place the coin at the top of the ramp as before. Let it go. Measure how far the coin travels. Record the measurement.

4 Take your book out of the pillowcase and use tape to stick the sheet of sandpaper to the front of your book. Use the book to create the ramp again. Place the coin at the top of the ramp and let it go. Does it slide? Measure and record the distance. On which of the three materials did the coin travel farthest. Was your hypothesis correct?

I Hypothesize...

Maybe you've used sandpaper before, or you might have watched someone else use it. If you have, you might know that it is so rough it will rub little pieces off wood. Does this information help you make a hypothesis?

GARDEN SCIENCE

Hypotheses often come from things that we observe around us every day. A good example of this is the work of Gregor Mendel, who spent a lot of time working in a garden.

Mendel was interested in how plants or animals often look like their parents. Think about your family. Do you have your dad's eyes? Perhaps your brother looks like your grandfather? Why do you think this is?

▼ You can tell these people are related! But why do they look like each other? Mendel's observations helped him make a hypothesis about this question.

▲ Mendel spent a lot of time working in the monastery garden. He started to notice things about the peas he grew. This led him to make a very famous hypothesis!

Mendel started by making a hypothesis. It said that pea plants pass on **traits** to their **offspring**. Traits are things like shape, size, and color.

Then Mendel designed some experiments to test his idea. In more than 30,000 experiments, Mendel was able to prove his hypothesis. Based on the work he did with peas, Mendel was able to make other hypotheses about how traits are passed along in animals and humans.

MOVING ON

So you've looked at all your research and made your hypothesis. Now you have to prove whether you were right or wrong.

▼ Once you've made your hypothesis you can plan your experiment. A good experiment will prove whether your hypothesis is right or wrong.

▲ Remember, a good hypothesis is based on knowledge. So, get out there and start learning about the world around you!

The third step of the scientific method is all about planning your experiment. This is where you work out what sort of experiment you will need to do and how you're going to do it. There are a lot of things to think about, like where and when you will do it, and what kind of **equipment** you will need. Remember, a well-planned experiment will always prove something.

Take the time to make a plan, so your experiment doesn't end up in a trash can!

KEEPING A JOURNAL

Imagine you are baking a cake. You've had a really good idea for a recipe, and you think it's going to be delicious. If it is, you will definitely want to make it again. But how would you remember how to make it again? How would you remember exactly how much sugar you used, or how long you baked it for? You would write it down, of course! Just like cooks, scientists need notes. Their notes explain exactly how they did their experiment. This is called a **journal**.

A journal can be anything from a scrapbook, to a binder with lined paper, from a computer file, to a notepad. The important thing about a journal is that it is where scientists record everything about their experiments, from beginning to end.

▼ Make sure you write down your hypothesis in your journal. You can also save your notes in a file on your computer.

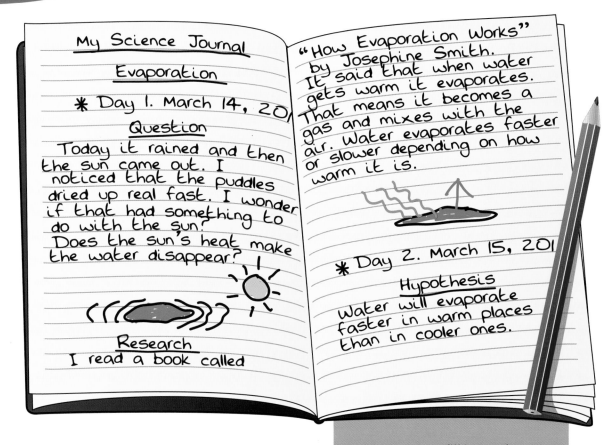

My Science Journal

Evaporation

* Day 1. March 14, 20?

Question

Today it rained and then the sun came out. I noticed that the puddles dried up real fast. I wonder if that had something to do with the sun? Does the sun's heat make the water disappear?

Research
I read a book called

"How Evaporation Works" by Josephine Smith. It said that when water gets warm it evaporates. That means it becomes a gas and mixes with the air. Water evaporates faster or slower depending on how warm it is.

* Day 2. March 15, 20?

Hypothesis
Water will evaporate faster in warm places than in cooler ones.

▲ Now you can fill in another stage of your journal. Make a careful note of your hypothesis. Remember to leave room for the next stage.

Here are Some Hot Tips for Keeping Your Journal:

- Make sure you write the date every time you use your journal;
- Make sure you write clearly, so that you'll be able to read your notes later on;
- Always write down any books, Web sites, or anything else you have used for research;
- Try writing a few sentences describing everything you have discovered in your research. This will help you think about it all and then make a hypothesis.

In this step of the scientific method, you can look through all the questions and information you've written in your journal so far. This will help you make your hypothesis.

TIMELINE

Below is a list of important and interesting hypotheses.

Year	Discovery or invention	Who made the hypothesis that led to the discovery or invention?
330 BC	Curved Earth	Archimedes observes that stars in southern countries are different from stars in countries further north. He hypothesizes that Earth is curved.
1667	The phlogiston hypothesis	Johann Becher hypothesizes that objects that burn contain something called phlogiston. He thinks fire is the phlogiston escaping as it gets hot. This hypothesis is later disproved.
1752	Lightning is static electricity	Benjamin Franklin hypothesizes that lightning is a kind of static electricity. He does a daring experiment to prove it.
1831	The theory of evolution	Charles Darwin sets off on a huge sea voyage to study rocks and animals. What he discovers leads him to make a very important hypothesis about the way **species** change over time.
1915	Continental drift	Alfred Wegener hypothesizes that the continents drift very slowly from one place to another. His hypothesis becomes a theory in the 1960s.
1974	Shark repellent	Eugenie Clark observes that a liquid from the Moses Sole makes her fingers tingle. She hypothesizes that it will work as shark repellent. It does!
Today	Life on Mars	Some scientists believe that there is life on the planet Mars. There is some evidence for this hypothesis. But there isn't enough for it to be a theory. In the future, scientists may find more evidence.

GLOSSARY

astronomy The scientific study of stars and planets

chart A way of showing numbers in rows and columns. Also called a table.

continent A large bit of land, such as North America

data Scientific information

disk A flat, circular shape

dissolve When a solid mixes with a liquid and seems to disappear

equipment All the physical things you need to do your experiment

geology The study of rocks and the way Earth is made

graph A diagram that can illustrate the results of an experiment. A graph has one measurement along the bottom, and another up the side

hypothesis An educated guess about what an experiment will prove

journal A record of every step of an experiment

monk A man who leads a very religious life

observation Noticing something happening by using the five senses

offspring The children of a living thing

philosopher Someone who creates ideas about people and the world

physics The study of energy and the basic things that make up the universe

prediction When you say that you think that something is going to happen in the future

printer Someone who makes things like books or newspapers

research Finding out facts about something

results The information that comes from an experiment

scientific method The way to do an experiment properly

species A group of animals or plants that are similar, like dogs or daisies

statement When you say something is definite

static electricity A type of electricity that moves from one place to another

theory An idea that has a lot of evidence, but hasn't been proved

traits Certain things about something, like weight or color

volume How much space something takes up

FURTHER INFORMATION

Books

First Encyclopedia of Science, Rachel Firth, Usborne Books, December 2002

Investigating the Scientific Method with Max Axiom, Donald B. Lemke, Tod Smith, and Al Milgrom, Capstone Press, 2008

Web sites

science.howstuffworks.com/scientific-method.htm

www.sciencebuddies.org/mentoring/project_scientific_method.shtml

INDEX